The Twelve Steps are reprinted with permission oi _____ Services, Inc. (AAWS). Permission to reprint the Twelve Steps does not mean that AAWS has reviewed or approved the contents of this publication, or that AAWS necessarily agrees with the views expressed herein. AA is a program of recovery from alcoholism only – use of the Twelve Steps with programs and activities which are patterned after AA -, but which address other problems, or in any other non-AA context, does not imply otherwise.

Special Thanks

John Bradshaw for his support

Francis and Eileen for the life lessons they taught

My granddaughter Taylor for her 12yearold perspective and editing

Sabin for showing me miracles do happen

Graham Newhouse for editing and encouragement

Jenny Meadows for editing and support

James and Delia for giving my permission to write and publish

Scott for his support

Mary-o and Nicky for teaching me tolerance, love and forgiveness

The teens I've worked with and known in recovery & the kids at a boarding school in Conroe, for helping me heal my inner teenager and showing me some issues most prevalent in teens.

The 12step approach, The SMART Recovery Program, books and training in grief work & time line therapy

Foreword by John Bradshaw

This book is excellent. It captures the language and needs of young people in a very powerful supportive way. Michael Yeager went directly to the heart of the matter when he translated some of the 12 steps into "young person" friendly language. Young people in recovery need to be spoken to in their own language and this book does just that!

The workbook layout is marvelous. It gives readers a chance to discover for themselves who and what they are. Their relation to their addictive disorder, and in turn their recovery, becomes clear. I am impressed with the way all addictive disorders are included in the text. Treating the disease of addiction as a whole is so much more powerful than just focusing on one addictive, problematic behavior at one time.

Yeager's workbook steps are "a report of action taken." They move people into life. They do not merely focus on moving them out of addictive behaviors. The process calls for writing their interpretation of the steps. Thus the person in recovery can discover for themselves who they are and how they have been refusing to be in relationship with themselves. As this is being done they can be guided into who they want to become, into entering into a relationship with themselves. The self-discovery starts a creative progression that is filled with possibility and new life experiences.

The chapter on challenging and changing core beliefs gets to the absolute center of all addictive, self-destructive behaviors. This work assists the young person in noticing first off what their "self-talk" is. Most kids have never really been taught to stand up to or for themselves. This work helps them do just that. I've heard addicts of all types say they did not like authority figures. Yeager's workbook clearly assists getting them to stand up to the biggest authority figure in their lives: themselves. Becoming conscious of their "self-talk" that drives their behavior leads to being able to change the talk, and change the behavior, away from addictive patterns. The exercises guide them in a process to take their power back and attach new more truthful meaning to what has happened in their lives. This is very strong work to remediate a strong disease.

Lastly, working on grief and saying goodbye to the pain in life is so necessary but is so often left undone. This book guides the young person to let go of their relationship to chemicals, addictive behaviors, past traumas, people who are no longer in their lives, attitudes, beliefs, behaviors, or previous identities.. With Yeager's workbook, once one has identified what needs to be said, and they say it, all that is left is to say goodbye.

I wholeheartedly recommend this book. I see it as a valuable tool for the young people themselves, counselors, ministers, parents and treatment programs working with young people. Anyone who does the work in this book will surely benefit.

John Bradshaw

CD and DVD Lectures and Workshop Collection
 www.johnbradshaw.com

Table of Contents

Chapter I		7
Chapter II	Step 1	14
Chapter III	Step 2	33
Chapter IV	Step 3	45
Chapter V	Step 4	57
Chapter VI	Step 5	71
Chapter VII	Step 6	77
Chapter VIII	Step 7	87
Chapter IX	Step 8	94
Chapter X	Step 9	101
Chapter XI	Step 10	112
Chapter XII	Step 11	125
Chapter XIII	Step 12	136
Chapter XIV	Challenging & Changing	
	Negative Self-Defeating Beliefs	147
Chapter XV	Grief/Loss Life Transitions	155
References, Training, Resources		171

Twelve + Two Steps

Young People

Recovery

Copyright © 8/15/08

by

Michael Yeager B.A., LCDC, C.Ht, RMT, CAS, CTC, SAP

Personally and professionally in the addiction recovery field since 1973

Chapter 1

This workbook is being written to be used by young people who are in recovery from any type of addiction, co-dependency, rage/angry outbursts or other dysfunctional behavior. It is taken from the 12 steps of Alcoholics Anonymous, as well as other adaptations of the 12 steps, and written in language understandable by young people. The text is meant to be used as a recovery tool for all addictive disorders. We will address alcohol, drugs other than alcohol, sex, gambling, spending, relationship, co-dependency, eating disorders, addiction etc. The steps will also be used to assist young people to resolve their problems around anger outbursts; depression; abandonment; family dysfunction; incest; sexual, physical, emotional, spiritual and financial abuse; low self-esteem; problematic behavior, as well as their sense of isolation and shame.

My working definition for addiction is borrowed from the World Health Organization. It states that, "Addiction is a recurring pathological relationship with a person, place, thing or event with life-damaging consequences." It's not what or how often a person engages in the behavior; it's what happens to them over a period of time that defines addiction. Problems get worse, not better, over a period of time. The thing to remember is that if you are addicted, your personal feelings about it will not change the fact that you are an addict. Complete and total abstinence, one day at time, is the answer when it comes to drug and alcohol recovery. There is a physical difference in our bodies that so far has not responded to any medical treatment. This is why it is called *an incurable terminal illness* if left untreated. This is also why being and staying completely clean, sober & addiction-free is required.

It does not matter how young or old you are. If you have the disease of addiction you will have to deal with treating it for the rest of your life, one day at a time. You may or may not continue with a 12-step program, but you must stay honest about your physical condition (i.e., your addiction) and remain clean and sober as well as away from your other addictive behaviors. You must also be aware of your motives for engaging in sex, spending, eating, relationships, exercise or other behaviors. It has also been suggested by many in recovery, that if you are a problem gambler you must remain abstinent from gambling as well.

Some may think they are too young to have a problem with addiction. Well, that is what this book is all about. It is designed to help you determine whether you are an addict or not. Honesty is the key in this process. <u>If you are honest and find that you are an addict, then you can handle it by treating it.</u>

John's Story

I used alcohol and other drugs from February 1963 to December 1973, from age 14 to 23, and I used cigarettes from 1967 to 1979. In both cases I used enough to cause physical problems that have had a long-term effect on my health. I have hepatitis and a breathing problem. I have also used sex, spending and excessive work to help avoid feelings. My story is not really unusual, and it's only my story, so it is personal and meaningful to me. It may have no meaning to you, yet I do hope it has some benefit for you.

I grew up in a dysfunctional family with an alcoholic father who was verbally and physically abusive. My mother did not have much of an ability to protect us from him or his anger and rage. I have become convinced that both of them did their best, regardless of how good or bad it was. I had a lot of bad feelings about myself and was an angry kid as well, with no positive outlets of expression. My father sobered up when I was 10 years old. He was verbally and physically abusive whether he was drunk or sober, and his personality did not change much, especially in his early years of sobriety. He continued to kick us boys 'til I was in the 8th grade. His verbal abuse lasted, though greatly diminished, 'til he died in 1990. He was a retired Marine sergeant who never really learned how to express his emotions, other than anger. Of course I am only making assumptions about him as he never told me these things about himself. The above is only my perception.

My behavior during my first 11 years was angry, quiet, combative, defiant, and argumentative. I had some friends but really saw myself as a loner. I joined the "Ugly Club" at a local radio station as this reflected how I felt about myself. I failed the 4th grade, which was just after my father sobered up. I changed my name when I transferred schools and did my second 4th – grade experience. I had my parents change it legally in the 8th grade. I was mean to my siblings and felt totally separated from them and the world. My drinking and drug use were to help change the way I felt and kill my emotional pain.

I got off drugs other than alcohol in August of 1972 and off the sedative drug alcohol in December 1973. For that I am grateful. I stopped a 4.5-pack-a-day cigarette habit in 1979. My use of sex, spending, and work as ways to medicate my feelings has greatly diminished. I'm glad it's a program of progress and not perfection.

I began by using alcohol as an altar boy in the Catholic Church. We would steal some wine when we did a mass or other church service. I did not drink much, but I did start in about the 3rd grade. In February of 1963 I went on a 90-mile horse ride in conjunction with the Houston rodeo. The cowboys helped me get my first real drink, and I got drunk that first night and 2 other nights on the 5-day ride. I did not like my hangovers, but I did like the getting-drunk part of it. By my junior year in High School, I used drugs other than alcohol. I began with marijuana then got into psychedelics and eventually fixing speed. In 1972 I quit using speed because I got hepatitis and went into the hospital. This scared me and I quit taking drugs other than alcohol. That was August 1, 1972. I continued to drink 'til December 13, 1973, and I quit drinking because I got very close to shooting speed again. I've been clean and sober since then. I stopped smoking cigarettes in 1979 because my 4.5-pack-a-day smoking habit was killing me.

In 1972 I entered a hospital with hepatitis from dirty needles and was really scared by the experience as I had never been sick before. I was off drugs other than alcohol as I knew I was out of control with drugs but I did not want my father's problems so I believed I was not alcoholic. I later found out that with addiction my wanting it or not wanting it does not matter. In October or November of 1972, after an AA conference, a friend of mine and I found out about NA, or Narcotics Anonymous, and we wanted to start a group. We went to Dallas and got the initial information, brought it back to Houston, and found a hospital to give us space to begin the first group in Houston. We were not willing to do just an AA thing at the time as both of us used drugs other than alcohol. I was also going to therapy at St. Joseph's Hospital 5 days a week, 2 group therapy sessions a day. I am a firm believer in combining 12-step work with therapy - whenever the need arises. This idea is consistent with the 12-step movement as it states, "be willing to go to any lengths." Therapy has helped me address the "causes and conditions" that set me up for my psychological problems that led me to believe I needed to medicate my feelings and harm my relationship with myself and others. My definition of addiction is "one's refusal to be in relationship with one's self." That is how I began my journey into recovery, and my life is pretty good now. The program taught me how to deal with life in an effective way.

So the remainder of the text is dedicated to a workbook that will guide you through the steps. Honesty is the key in this process. You are the one who benefits most by doing this work. You alone will die or live an uncomfortable life if you do not change your lifestyle. It's to bad you are young with this problem. So get on with recovery now and stop wasting time complaining about it or denying it any longer. A young dog can learn new tricks. Like it or not, it's your life. The question is: What do you want to do with it?

NOTES

NOTES

Chapter 2

Step 1

We admitted we were powerless over _____, that our lives had become unmanageable or out of control.

Or

We admitted we could not control or predict our behavior after we started (using, acting out, raging, drinking, having sex, gambling, spending, exercising, eating, binging/purging, etc). **Fill in the blank_____ with your behavior or behaviors.**

Or

We admitted we were powerless over our addictive, self-destructive behavior and that our lives had become unmanageable and out of control.

Alcohol, drugs, sexual acting out, gambling, work, relationships, compulsive spending, over- or under-eating, bulimia, anorexia etc., and other addictive co-dependent behavior can be the things the first step is talking about. Just fill in the blank with the one or ones that fit for you.

Truthfully and candidly explain what happens when you engage in the above behaviors. Addiction gets worse, not better, over time. What type of problems exists now that did not exist when you began using?

Money problems

_____

_____

_____

_____

_____

_____

_____

_____

Family problems

_____

_____

_____

_____

_____

_____

_____

Sexual problems

_____

_____

_____

_____

_____

_____

School problems

_____

_____

_____

_____

_____

_____

_____

Relationship problems

_____

_____

_____

_____

_____

_____

_____

Legal problems

_____

_____

_____

_____

_____

_____

_____

_____

Self-esteem problems

_____

_____

_____

_____

_____

_____

_____

_____

Other problem areas

_____

_____

_____

_____

_____

_____

_____

_____

_____

People with beginning-, middle- or late-stage addiction seem to make promises to themselves and/or others that they can't or don't keep. It's like saying "I promise myself that I will not get into trouble today or tonight when I use (name the behavior)" and then they end up in some type of trouble with themselves or others. The addict/alcoholic does not seem to be able to reliably predict their behavior after they start using.

For the other addictive (process addictions i.e. sex, gambling, spending, eating, work, relationships, love, rage, or problematic behaviors, the addict seems to continue to get caught up in the addictive behavior even if it causes problems. Problems

like eating or spending to kill off or to repress some feeling, or getting into relationships that don't work, over and over again.

It's helpful to know when your using behavior changed from experimental to a problem, or when you became dependent upon it.

When did you notice the change?

_____

_____

_____

_____

_____

_____

_____

_____

_____

_____

_____

When did you notice you began to change friends, and were the new friendships based on drugs, alcohol, sex, relationship, eating, not-eating, love, anger, rage, (blaming self, parents, law, school, society for problems), etc.?

_____

_____

_____

_____

_____

_____

How did you notice or become aware of problems caused by your using behavior? Did your parents, school, the law, or friends tell or confront you about your using behavior? Or did you notice your own behavior?

_____

_____

_____

_____

_____

When did you notice you were having problems concentrating, and getting along with others? When did you change your appearance, personal hygiene and grades?

_____

_____

_____

_____

_____

_____

When did you notice you increased your chemical intake or dysfunctional behavior to get the same results? A decrease in the amount you take to get the same results?

_____

_____

_____

_____

_____

_____

When did you notice you needed to increase the levels of excitement in your life by engaging in more or different kinds of sex, relationships, gambling, eating, not-eating, anger, rage, etc.?

_____

_____

_____

_____

_____

_____

Describe the kind and types of problems caused by your behavior.

_____

_____

_____

_____

_____

_____

If you were involved in sports or extra-curricular activities, when did you stop doing them or lose interest in them and start using your addictive or compulsive behavior?

_____

_____

_____

_____

_____

_____

Dr. Patrick Carnes, in his book titled "*Out of the Shadows,*" a text written to treat sexual addiction, describes the cycle of addiction. I will define the cycle then ask you to answer some questions to see how you fit into the cycle.

The first phase in the cycle is called acting according to your belief system. It describes the primary beliefs that the addict thinks are true about self. The beliefs have to do with one's relationship with self and others.

The first belief is "I'm basically a bad, unworthy person"-,

The second is "No one would love me as I am"-,

The third is "I can't depend on others to be here for me"

And the fourth is "Alcohol, drugs, sex, relationships, eating, not-eating, gambling, spending, acting out with anger/rage or the addictive/compulsive behavior is my most important need."

To notice how you are affected by your beliefs, it's important to define them for yourself. Basically it's important to know what the beliefs mean to you. What are your negative, limiting beliefs about yourself?

_____

_____

_____

_____

_____

_____

_____

_____

_____

_____

The second phase of the cycle is the impaired thinking that goes along with addictive/compulsive behaviors. This impaired thinking keeps the person involved with their addictive/compulsive behavior and must be broken through before recovery can happen. The Big Book of AA indicates that one must really accept the fact that their addictive behavior is a problem. SMART recovery also states that it is necessary for the addict to tell the truth about their relationship with the addictive behavior before recovery happens. The impaired thinking is as follows:

Denial

Dishonesty

Delusion

Distortion

Defensiveness

Despair

Let's go over these one at a time to see how they apply to your life.

Denial means that you acted as if what is happening is not happening. How have you denied your using/angry/co-dependent/addictive behavior?

_____

_____

_____

_____

_____

_____

_____

Dishonesty means that one is just not truthful. It could also mean that someone creates a story. The story often describes how much or how often a person uses, as well as what happens when they use, and is not accurate about the effects of the usage.

_____

_____

_____

_____

_____

_____

_____

Delusion means to hold on to a belief even though it is false. For example, if you believed you were a king, but no one else thought you were a king, you would have a delusion of grandeur. What are your delusions (false beliefs) about your addictive or compulsive behavior?

_____

_____

_____

_____

_____

_____

Distortion means to give an inaccurate or misleading account of something, to misrepresent something-, or an aspect of yourself. How have you misrepresented some aspect of your addictive/compulsive/acting-out behavior?

_____

_____

_____

_____

_____

Defensiveness is focusing attention on others, their roles, responsibilities and behaviors, while not letting anyone get too close or see too much of you. In order to maintain defensiveness, you might manipulate, project, blame, rage, lie, bully, run away, leave, act like a victim, argue, etc. How are you defensive?

_____

_____

_____

_____

_____

_____

_____

_____

_____

_____

_____

Despair is the feeling of hopelessness that things can't or won't change. Despair is the sense that you are not in control, and the sense that you are unwilling to let go of control you don't even have. How do you live in despair?

_____

_____

_____

_____

_____

_____

_____

_____

_____

_____

_____

_____

_____

_____

_____

_____

The next phase in the cycle of addiction is preoccupation. Preoccupation is an intense thought that prevents you from focusing on other thoughts. When you live in preoccupation, you tune out everything else to keep your mind on that one thing. An addict typically thinks about the last time or times he/she used, or on the opportunity to use next time. This preoccupation process also keeps the person away from the pain caused by the above two activities. What thoughts preoccupy your time?

_____

_____

_____

_____

_____

_____

The next phase leads to the first set of behaviors used in the cycle. The first three were thought processes. **Now we get to behavior, Ritualization**.

Rituals are how you usually dress when you act out, where you go to get high or do your addictive behavior, the time of day you typically do the addictive/compulsive activity, whom you do the activity with, the kind or type of cologne or perfume you wear, the color of nail polish you use, type of alcohol you drink, drugs you use, race track you hang out on, gambling activity you typically do, foods you avoid or eat, etc.

What is the ritual you do just prior to your using, acting out, etc?

_____

_____

_____

_____

_____

_____

_____

_____

_____

The final phase is the addictive/compulsive/acting-out behavior. What are one or more typical behaviors you do when you use?

_____

_____

_____

_____

_____

_____

Addiction causes problems most or all of the time. Now let's look for its emotional costs to you in the form of despair. What are your feelings typically after you use or engage in the addictive/compulsive action or behavior?

_____

_____

_____

_____

_____

_____

And finally let's look at the unmanageability in your life as a result of using or doing your behavior. How is your life more complicated or problematic as a result of using?

_____

_____

_____

_____

_____

_____

All in all, we are looking for the effects of using. How does your use affect how you view yourself? What is your self-talk before, during and after using or participating in your addictive behavior?

_____

_____

_____

_____

_____

How do your addictive behavior and your beliefs impact or change your relationships with others?

_____

_____

_____

_____

_____

_____

_____

_____

How does your addiction impact your ability to get your needs met?

_____

_____

_____

_____

_____

_____

_____

How does your addictive behavior "define" your life?

_____

_____

_____

_____

_____

_____

_____

_____

The first step in recovery is simply telling the truth about what happens when you use or are getting ready to use. The truth is not easy to see. It's hard to admit that your addiction or-, co-dependent behavior causes you to act "out of control."

How has your "out of control" behavior impacted your life?

_____

_____

_____

_____

_____

_____

Is there anything else you can say to truthfully explain the problems in your life that result from your addiction? If so, write it down now.

_____

_____

_____

_____

_____

NOTES

NOTES

Chapter 3

Step *2*
"Came to believe that a Power greater than ourselves could restore us to sanity."

***Or** it could be said this way:*

"Came to believe that a Higher Power could help us return to normal living without so many problems."

Or

"We decided to take charge of our lives, with the help of a Higher Power, and act and think our way into a permanent way of right acting and thinking."

Some have discounted the "Higher Power" or "God" idea because of past life events. Some attach a negative association to God and see this being like some unfriendly authority figure or an abusive father or mother figure. Others have no beliefs about this power one way or another.

The importance of God or a "Higher Power" in the 12-step approach is to give you power in your lives over the addiction or problem behavior. Armed with a positive relationship with a Higher Power, you can begin to act sanely by first remaining clean, sober, or without using your other addictive behavior, having angry outbursts, or depression. Getting addiction-free is just the beginning. The real trick is to stay that way regardless of what happens. Believing in a "Higher Power" has helped many to stay addiction-free.

By believing in a power greater than yourself you can begin to make the choice to turn to **it** instead of your old addictive acting-out behavior when cravings to use or act out come up. As you begin to develop this relationship, usually because you were desperate for some type of help, you begin to see that this power is there for you. In some cases this is the first time you've noticed this. Some of you believed you were in this world alone with no one to help you. Addiction has also been called the disease of isolation. Years ago, in a piece of literature about being consumed by addiction, there was a drawing with a man crawling out of a bottle. He had been isolated from the world by his addictive behavior and was now climbing out of that isolation.

If the whole God or Higher Power idea is just too much for you, please do not think that it is absolutely necessary to believe in order for you to recover. What is important is that you find for yourself something to believe in that has more power than you do that will help you make the necessary changes to stay addiction-free. When using and acting out, you used something more powerful than you (drugs, alcohol, sex, gambling, spending, anger, rage, food, and exercise) to help you change your feelings. You can find a replacement power to help you live an addiction-free life.

Alcohol, drugs, and/or your addictive acting-out behavior caused you to be isolated from the world in the following ways:

_____

_____

_____

_____

_____

_____

You gave up on yourself and lost trust in others in the following ways:

_____

_____

_____

_____

_____

_____

_____

The second step provides an opportunity to create a relationship with a God, Higher Power or our Higher Self if you don't like the God concept. A man I knew years ago, George T, called GOD (*Good Orderly Direction*) and said to find anything that can help you get that going in your life and believe in it. We are talking about spirituality, not religion. Religion tells its believers what to believe and how to define God. So religion is exclusive whereas spirituality is inclusive because it says to find something you can believe in, and then place your faith in it so you can find solutions to your problems and live a happy life.

So when Step 2 says "… came to believe," it means that you can open your minds and hearts to something bigger than you are that will "restore you to sanity." In the beginning, sanity is simply clean, sober, non-acting-out behavior. It is also having thoughts and actions that empower you rather than take your power away.

So it's helpful to begin this step by reviewing how you used to believe in God, Higher Power or Higher Self, prior to using, or acting out. Then you can examine how you believe now that you have decided to stop using or acting out, and whether you think this power can help you.

Your relationship with God, Higher Power, Higher Self prior to using/acting out was like this:

_____

_____

_____

_____

_____

_____

_____

During your using/acting-out behavior your God, Higher Power, or Higher Self was …

_____

_____

_____

_____

_____

_____

Now that you have decided to stop using or acting out, your God, Higher Power, Higher Self is …

_____

_____

_____

_____

_____

_____

_____

This is just the beginning of this new relationship. It will grow and change as you grow and change. The other 10 steps help you take the action necessary to develop this relationship with your God, Higher Power or Higher Self. Faith without works is dead, so action is the key to living your faith and trusting your Higher Power. When using or acting out, it's your actions that produced results like getting in trouble, etc. So when you change, it's your actions that help you get out of trouble and/or to live happier lives.

Since you know how you used to believe in God, it can be helpful to determine what you want to believe about God now. Since you are beginning this new relationship, why not decide on how you want your God to act if you are going to be in relationship with him/her/it?

It's time now for you to decide who your God, Higher Power or Higher Self is. Your Higher Power acts like this:

_____

_____

_____

_____

_____

_____

God in the second step is being called on to "restore me to sanity." This indicates you must have been acting insane in order for you to need a Higher Power to restore you to sanity. You have been acting insane using/acting out in the following ways:

_____

_____

_____

_____

_____

Your thinking regarding your ability to successfully use has been insane in the following ways:

_____

_____

_____

_____

_____

_____

Insane actions continue as long as impaired thinking occurs. Impaired thinking includes denial, delusion, rationalization, minimization and justification. You identified these stages in the first step. Review them now.

Step 2 states you will be restored to sanity as a result of your belief in a Higher Power, God, or your Higher Self. When you sanity is restored you will act and think like:

_____

_____

_____

_____

_____

Part of the insanity of addiction, co-dependency, or acting out is the belief that the next time you "do the behavior" you will act differently, better, or changed somehow. How have you had this insane belief? What were your beliefs?

_____

_____

_____

_____

_____

_____

_____

_____

_____

_____

_____

To be restored to sanity in this area you have to change your thinking and your actions in some way. Explain how you plan to do this.

_____

_____

_____

_____

_____

_____

In order for you to be able to believe in your God, Higher Power, or Higher Self, it is helpful, if you are teachable and open. How are you willing to let this happen?

_____

_____

_____

_____

_____

_____

You know what you were originally taught about a God concept. Write it down now like you remember it.

_____

_____

_____

_____

_____

_____

_____

_____

_____

_____

_____

_____

_____

_____

_____

Has that belief served you or been useful to you in any way? Explain your answer.

_____

_____

_____

_____

_____

_____

_____

_____

_____

_____

_____

_____

_____

_____

_____

In recovery it's helpful to define exactly what you now believe or are willing to believe in. Write out how you want this God, Higher Power, or Higher Self to be for you.

_____

_____

_____

_____

_____

_____

Because you have created this belief that you say works, or could work for you, how do you plan to use it to help you now?

_____

_____

_____

_____

_____

_____

NOTES

NOTES

Chapter 4

Step 3

"We turned our will and our lives over to the care of our Higher Power as we understood Him."

Or

"We decided to rely on our Higher Power to help in all areas of our lives."

Or

"We decided to let our Higher Power help in all areas of our lives."

This step states that you now trust this power to be here for you and you can rely on it. By the time you take this step you have had time to test out this power to see exactly how it will work. The reliance on this power source instead of defiance of this power source is in place, and you can be more in touch with your growing relationship with this source.

If you admitted your powerlessness over alcohol, chemicals, other people, past events, and other addictive behaviors, how does this prepare you for the third step?

_____

_____

_____

_____

_____

Step 3 is an action step. You are asked to make a decision to turn your will (thoughts) and lives (actions) over to the care of your power source. This is the foundation that supports the remaining steps. You are making a decision to turn to your Higher Power when you are in trouble, or are seeking answers. It is also asking you to demonstrate your belief in your Higher Power to do for you what you have not been able to do for yourself. This is a hard step because it is difficult to let go of your illusion of control you thought you had in your lives. It means you are going to give your will and lives to your Higher Power's care. It may seem like a good thing, but to do it requires intense trust in your Higher Power to take care of you.

You have difficulty trusting others because...

_____

_____

_____

_____

_____

_____

Specifically you have the following trust issues with your father:

_____

_____

_____

_____

_____

_____

_____

_____

With your mother:

_____

_____

_____

_____

_____

_____

_____

_____

_____

With your brother/s:

_____

_____

_____

_____

_____

_____

_____

With your sister/s:

_____

_____

_____

_____

_____

_____

_____

With authority figures:

_____

_____

_____

_____

_____

_____

_____

With yourself (you have made promises to yourself and have not kept them):

_____

_____

_____

_____

_____

_____

How did you learn=about a God or Higher Power in family, church, friends or school?

_____

_____

_____

_____

_____

_____

_____

Your God or Higher Power means:

_____

_____

_____

_____

_____

_____

_____

_____

In order to do Step 3 successfully, you must check out your willingness to let go of your illusion of control. Living this step suggests you give your Higher Power all of you. You hold nothing back. To do this step requires willingness to do this over and over again, possibly many times throughout the day. So you are choosing to trust your personal relationship with your Higher Power to enable you to take the necessary action to clean up your lives and help you keep your lives in order. Your willingness also comes as your intention to give your Higher Power a chance to work with you. You are, in effect, choosing to trust this power to be here for you. Some of you did not have parents, family, or friends who were there when you needed them. Now, in recovery, you are reworking your concepts. What appeared true when using or acting out is no longer true in this new life you are choosing. New life means new choices and perceptions. What was true when using or action out is no longer the truth.

How do you mistrust anything or anyone to be there for you?

_____

_____

_____

_____

_____

_____

_____

Since you've started living the 12 steps in your life, how have others been here for you?

_____

_____

_____

_____

_____

_____

_____

What proof do you have that your Higher Power is in your life helping you?

_____

_____

_____

_____

_____

_____

_____

My understanding of God or my Higher Power is…

_____

_____

_____

_____

_____

_____

_____

The first part of this step says "Make a decision," which means you think about something and, from all the information you have available at the time; you choose a direction or way of thinking. This means that your thinking is being restored to sanity because you are asking for help and support to manage your lives in a more positive way. This step is a step in trust as well. By making the decision to turn over your will and your lives, you have studied the pros and cons, and the decision seems like a good one.

List your good points (pros) and bad points (cons) that led you to make this decision:

_____

_____

_____

_____

_____

_____

_____

"To turn our will and our lives over to the care of our Higher Power or Higher Self"
means different things to people, depending on the person-, and how they believe.
What does it mean to you?

_____

_____

_____

_____

_____

_____

Some people believe that you are deciding to rely on your Higher Power to help in
your thinking "will." The Big Book of AA states that your problem "centers in your
minds." Your minds are where your brains are, and your thinking comes from there.
So you have decided to believe that your Higher Power, Higher Self will do a better
job with your thinking than you have done. Do you play victim to people, places,
things, or events? Do you make statements like "He/she made me feel or do_____?"
If so, write your victim statement.

_____

_____

_____

Describe how you could benefit from changed thinking.

_____

_____

_____

_____

_____

_____

_____

Now what about your lives? This means how you act in public and private. "How you act" means everything you do: How you dress, whom you associate with, how you progress in work-, or school, how you act with your family and friends, the types of life responsibilities you take on or not, and how you express your feelings or not. Your actions are:

_____

_____

_____

_____

Does anger manage you, or do you manage it?

_____

_____

_____

_____

_____

_____

_____

The final part of Step 3 is "As we understood Him."

How did you understand God, and how has your understanding changed?

_____

_____

_____

_____

_____

_____

How can you use your Higher Power in your daily life?

_____

_____

_____

_____

_____

_____

_____

_____

_____

It has been stated that the 3rd-step has little to no lasting value unless it is immediately followed by a thorough Step 4. It is suggested that once you complete your third step, you immediately begin writing your life inventory. Remember, you are armed with your Higher Power, which you have just turned you will and life over to. The work of the 3rd-step sets you up to feel empowered to tell the truth about your lives. This is what Step 4 is all about.

NOTES

NOTES

Chapter 5

Step 4

"Made a searching and fearless moral inventory of ourselves".

Or

"Looked at the bad and good in ourselves in a non-judgmental way".

Or

"Decided to enter into a truthful relationship with ourselves by writing down the truth about our behavior ".

This step involves telling the truth about you. Most addicts, alcoholics and those of you with other addictive acting-out behaviors did not tell much or any of the truth when involved in your addictive acting-out behaviors. The willingness to do this work, for some of you, came simply from fear. Fear that if you did not do this work you might return to your old behaviors. For some of you the motivation was a parent, peer, or sponsor. You thought that if you did the work they would leave you alone. Some of you had to give up the idea that your business was just that, your business, and no one else had the right to know it. Another idea for many is that telling about it will not do any thing about it. Some of you came from violent or abusive families, and it may be difficult to keep the focus on doing your own inventory not theirs. You can use God or your concept of a Higher Power to do for you what is hard to do for yourself. By practicing steps 1, 2, & 3 again and again, you can do the work of Step 4 as well as the other steps. Remember the steps are reports of actions taken by others before you that helped them to change their lives.

When thinking about doing Step 4, your greatest discomfort with it is…

_____

_____

_____

_____

_____

_____

You hesitate to do the 4th Step because…

_____

_____

_____

_____

_____

_____

Your anxieties about doing Step 4 are…

_____

_____

_____

_____

_____

_____

Your family's rules about discussing your feelings or things that you've done, or things that have happened to you are:

_____

_____

_____

_____

_____

_____

Even though Step 4 is not about telling anything to anybody, Step 5 is about sharing what you have written with someone else. How are you projecting your feelings onto the future, and how is this stopping you or holding you back from doing the work of Step 4?

_____

_____

_____

_____

_____

_____

Step 4 can also help you overcome fears of admitting things that you have done or the part you played in your own messed-up lives. What fears are alive and well in your life that relate to your telling these truths?

_____

_____

_____

_____

Resentment, the holding on to or re-feeling of old anger issues, causes a lot of problems. A powerful aspect of this step is that you get to begin to let go of this anger,-, or resentment as a demonstration of your taking your life back. If you resent something or someone, the resentment controls you. In Step 4 you get your power back by seeing the part you play in the situation. This is hard sometimes to see the part you have played. The following process may help you.

Make 4 columns. In the first column write down:

(1) The name of the person, place, thing or event that is troubling you

(2) What happened to you

(3) How it affected you

(4) The part you played in the situation. This last column is meant to help you see your part in how you reacted to, internalized, or brought about the event. Shame or blame are not the idea here; rather, just a realistic look at what has happened and the part you played.

Resentment Inventory List

For example:

(1)	(2)	(3)	(4)
Father	Hit me; called me stupid	Lost self-esteem	Held onto pain/lost boundaries

Create an inventory for all the persons, places, things or events that have troubled you. Some of you have done this process with each separate set of issues; i.e., what you want to do is to focus on all your relationships to people, places, things and events that you have uncomfortable feelings about. This gets you to the causes and conditions that set you up for addictive, co-dependent, acting-out behavior. Your inventory helps you identify the problems you have been carrying around all this time. These problems cause emotional pain, and if the pain is not released you return to pain killers; i.e., drugs, alcohol, rage, sex, gambling, codependency, blaming, spending, or acting out in whatever way you can to numb the feelings. Listed below are some areas you can create an inventory about. If your issues are not listed, just add them, and do the work.

It's important to remember that resentment is the Number 1 offender of the addict. Resentment, more than anything else, seems to drive the addict back into destructive, addictive, co-dependent behavior. Sometimes it's helpful to start with a list. List everything and every event that goes with each issue listed below. Once that is completed, do the 4-column exercise with each relationship or issue.

You feel angry about…

_____

_____

_____

_____

_____

_____

_____

_____

_____

You feel resentment about…

_____

_____

_____

_____

_____

_____

_____

_____

Sex problems and partners....

_____

_____

_____

_____

_____

Relationships…

_____

_____

_____

_____

_____

_____

_____

Love…

_____

_____

_____

_____

_____

_____

_____

_____

Fear has run your life in the following ways…

_____

_____

_____

_____

_____

_____

_____

Approval-seeking …

_____

_____

_____

_____

_____

_____

How you control…

_____

_____

_____

_____

_____

_____

_____

How you've abandoned yourself and how other have abandoned you, and what you made up about that for yourself…

_____

_____

_____

_____

_____

_____

Sexual Abuse/Incest …

_____

_____

_____

_____

_____

_____

Money …

_____

_____

_____

_____

_____

_____

_____

Other …

_____

_____

_____

_____

_____

_____

_____

_____

Being complete is important. Remember that whatever you do is appropriate for the inventory. Inventories are never perfect, but they are adequate and do get the job done. You can do the inventory many times, and each time it is just right. Remember, this is a tool for recovery. Some of you think you are perfectionists, so you will not do anything unless you believe you are going to do it right. Well, give yourself an "A" now, and accept that whatever you do is right for this time.

How have your perfectionist ideas gotten you in trouble in the past?

_____

_____

_____

_____

Do you ever say or think "If I can't do it right, why do it?" Or maybe you are the scapegoat who says "To hell with it." How have these attitudes affected you in the past? What goes on within you to set you up for these thoughts?

_____

_____

_____

_____

In some addicted or dysfunctional families, the family members are assigned roles. These roles are assigned but never discussed. The roles become the person's way of relating and behaving and the person believes they are the role. The classic roles are as follows. **The first-born is usually called the Family Hero**. This person usually does everything right and looks "good" for the family, usually a high achiever. If the "Hero" has a drug/alcohol or acting-out problem, it surprises the family, their teachers, friends, etc. **The next is the "Scapegoat"**, the one who is often in trouble. Trouble in school, legal problems, fighting or anger problems are the norm for this person. The family focuses on them as the problem in the family so the family can defocus on other problems. **The third role is the "Mascot".** This person is the family jokester. They make jokes out of many things, keeping it light. This gives the family comic relief for the problems in the family. **The last role is the "Lost Child."** This person is usually quiet, and basically unseen in the family. They are withdrawn and try to stay out of the problems. The roles are rigid and the family system does what ever it can to keep the roles in place. It is helpful in inventory work to identify the role you play in the system.

The primary role you play in the family is

_____

_____

_____

_____

_____

_____

You have identified yourself with this role in the following ways

_____

_____

_____

_____

_____

_____

_____

_____

Your inventory gives you the opportunity to see exactly where you are in your life. My own definition of addiction is "One's refusal to be in relationship with oneself."

List below the reasons that prevent you from establishing a truthful relationship with yourself.

_____

_____

_____

_____

_____

_____

_____

_____

_____

_____

Good luck and tell the truth.

NOTES

NOTES

Chapter 6

Step 5

"Admitted to God, ourselves and another human being the exact nature of our wrongs".

Or

"Told our Higher Power, ourselves and someone trustworthy the exact truth of where I was wrong".

Or

"Got honest with my Higher Power, myself, and someone I can trust by telling then what I wrote in the 4th step".

Here you share what you wrote with your Higher Power, yourself and a sponsor, counselor, priest/minister/rabbi/nun, or trusted friend. By sharing, you can recognize your patterns of behavior and emotional responses to life. There may be certain feelings that have held you back or stopped you from progressing in life. Notice it's not an "I'm wrong" list; rather it is a "looking for the exact nature of my wrongs" list.

Your patterns of behavior seem to be:

_____

_____

_____

_____

_____

_____

The value here is to see what motivated you to drink, act out, be angry, resentful, blame, keep feelings in, etc. When these underlying drivers of behavior are understood, you become free from the addictive or acting-out behaviors. The person hearing your step will be able to help you understand how these thoughts have gone along with your addictive and dysfunctional behaviors.

Behaviors and beliefs that accompany your drinking, drug, acting-out behaviors are:

_____

_____

_____

_____

_____

_____

_____

_____

_____

Step 5 also helps develop your relationship with your Higher Power and at least one other person. Many have called addiction a disease of isolation. Step 5 is a step out of isolation and into connections with others.

As a result of doing this step, you have increased your faith and trust in your God or Higher Power and other people in the following ways:

_____

_____

_____

_____

_____

In Step 5 one simply reads the inventory to their sponsor, counselor, clergy or trusted friend. The purpose is to acknowledge your events and experiences. No judgment is called for or desired. In fact negative self-judgment is often one of the character defects that may have already been identified. Staying away from shame, judgment, guilt, or remorse may require you to rely more and more on your Higher Power to restore you to sanity, because nothing is accomplished by judging yourself for past behaviors. Being held accountable for your behavior is healthy; being beaten up for it is not.

Another purpose of this step is to look for patterns of behavior and beliefs that drive your addictive, destructive behavior. You tell the truth about your lives and behavior, and share your truths with someone outside yourself who can be objective and help you see yourself in a different light. By telling your truths you can then take actions to stop them from recurring these actions are in Steps 6 & 7 so you can take your power back. Not power over alcohol or drugs, but power over your reactions to life events.

It is important to immediately take Step 5 right after you do Step 4. There is no benefit in holding on to the information from Step 4. The steps are action steps. They move you from pain to peacefulness and from regret to acceptance. The steps do not tell you what to avoid; they simply suggest what to do if you are going to live the program. In reality, you are always living some type of program. It is either the 12-step solution-based program, or a program that you lived prior to deciding to recover, or some other type of program or way of life. In your addiction there was no way out of problems. By working the steps, you are finding that you move out of your problem relationship with yourself, God, and others. So Step 5 helps you develop honesty, a quality many of you lacked when you used or blamed others. It also helps you develop trust in another person, and trust in God to be here for you. Many addicts, co-dependents, and alcoholics have a difficult time with trust. You trust in yourself and others. The lifestyles you lived did not foster trust either. Your using buddies were as untrustworthy as you were.

Thought and behavioral patterns identified by you and the person you take your 5th step with; i.e. the nature of your wrongs.

_____

_____

_____

_____

_____

_____

_____

_____

NOTES

NOTES

Chapter 7

Step 6

"We're entirely ready to have God recover all these defects of character".

Or

"Once I know the facts about me I am ready to have my Higher Power remove my flaws of character".

Your successful working of the first 5 steps indicates your readiness to complete Step 6. Now that you know the exact nature of your wrongs, the question is whether you want them gone. Step 6 gives you the opportunity to decide for yourself if you want to live without these defects of character. The step is like checks and balances. If you have been honest so far, and moving towards recovery, do you want to continue moving in that direction? If so, are you ready to have God do for you what you have not been able to do for yourself? If the answer is yes, then you are willing. If the answer is no, then go back to Step 4 to further inventory your lives to see the exact nature of your wrongs. It is your wrongs that keep you out of honest relationship with yourself, God, and others. If you want to hold onto some character defect, you will want to know whether it helps you recover or not. If the answer is that it does not, then are you willing to let God or your higher power help you let it go? It is this balance you go through in the 6th step that helps you move through the process.

List the areas in your life that still cause you to feel guilty, shameful, angry, etc. Are you aware of being ready to have God or your Higher Power remove these character defects?

You know you have let God have the following character defects:

_____

_____

_____

_____

_____

_____

_____

_____

The character traits identified are usually very deep and a part of your patterns of behavior. In many cases they are part of your life skills tools you have used unconsciously over and over again. The inventory makes you conscious of your behavior and the drivers for these behaviors.

As your awareness of these defects grows, and you accept them, you can ask your Higher Power for help in removing them. You can ask God to help you become ready to live without your defects.

You are anxious/uncomfortable when you think about living with out the following "survival tools" or behaviors identified in Step 4 that no longer work for you.

_____

_____

_____

_____

_____

_____

_____

_____

_____

_____

_____

What is your level of trust in your Higher Power when you consider your entire willingness to have these defects removed?

_____

_____

_____

_____

_____

What is your relationship to/with God or your Higher Power at this part of your program?

_____

_____

_____

_____

_____

What can you use to remind yourself that you decided to give these defects to God?

_____

_____

_____

_____

_____

_____

_____

Many people have found that after they discovered their character defects they were comfortable with some of them. The thought or idea that they would be removed was threatening.

Even though it is difficult, you are asking God or your Higher Power to help you become willing to let them go. In some cases all or part of your identity is tied up in your defects. By identity I mean how you talk, walk, dress, how you accept or reject reality and/or authority, who you hang out with, or how you relate to the world. You may be fearful or uncertain about how to act without your character defects. If you are, you can return to Step 2 and 3 to reaffirm your beginning dependence or reliance on a Higher Power. It will help you overcome your reluctance to give up your character defects.

You notice you are not entirely ready to let go of the following defects of character:

_____

_____

_____

_____

_____

_____

How are you tied up in your relationship with your character defects?

_____

_____

_____

_____

_____

_____

The defects you are not ready to let go of yet mean the following to you:

_____

_____

_____

_____

_____

_____

The step or actions you can take that will help you become willing are….

_____

_____

_____

_____

_____

_____

You know your God or Higher Power loves you just the way you are, defects and all! List exactly how you know this:

_____

_____

_____

_____

_____

_____

_____

The first 5 steps helped you get ready to give up your character defects in the following ways:

_____

_____

_____

_____

_____

_____

_____

You are confident that the steps will improve your quality of life in the following ways:

_____

_____

_____

_____

_____

_____

_____

_____

_____

_____

Faith that your Higher Power can and will prepare you for the removal of these defects requires humility. Humility is the knowledge that you do not know everything. So you trust that God or your Higher Power will guide you in removing the character defects that separate you from doing your highest good here on earth. You practice this by becoming ready for the defect to be removed.

You are inspired by the idea that God or your Higher Power will remove your defects of character in the following ways:

_____

_____

_____

_____

_____

_____

The experiences you've had so far that indicate you are making progress toward allowing God to remove these defects are:

_____

_____

_____

_____

_____

The Sixth Step states your willingness to have these defects removed. How can you live, or demonstrate, your willingness?

_____

_____

_____

_____

_____

Even if you do not know <u>how</u> they will be removed, are you now willing for them to be removed?

_____

_____

_____

_____

_____

If so, move onto the 7th Step.

NOTES

NOTES

Chapter 8

Step 7

"Humbly asked Him to remove our shortcomings".

Or

"Humbly asked my Higher Power to release me from my shortcomings.

Humility has nothing to do with humiliation. Humility means that you recognize that your power is limited and you need a power greater that yourself to help you. You are not looking down at yourself or your behavior. You are simply asking for something to be done for you that you find difficult or impossible to do for yourself. You are practicing your growing belief in reliance on your Higher Power rather than your defiance of your Higher Power.

Humility means...

_____

_____

_____

_____

_____

_____

_____

_____

_____

_____

How have you already practiced humility in working the previous 6 steps?

_____

_____

_____

_____

_____

_____

The following examples show how you are focusing less on yourself and more on your God or your Higher Power.

_____

_____

_____

_____

_____

_____

_____

In AA the Seventh Step prayer is a powerful statement of this process. It reads, "My Creator, I am now willing that you should have all of me, good and bad. I pray that you now remove from me every single defect of character which stands in the way of my usefulness to you and my fellows. Grant me strength, as I go out from here, to do your bidding. Amen"

It's a short and sweet prayer. You have done a lot of work to get to this point. You have told the truth about your relationship to chemicals and other addictive destructive behaviors, and come to believe that a Higher Power could help. You turned your life over to its care, then did a written inventory, shared it, and became willing to have the defects removed. Now you are just letting it all go. This is your last step in grieving your old lifestyle and/or behavior. Letting go is not hard to do at this point on your journey.

Your resistance to letting God or your Higher Power take these defects is:

_____

_____

_____

_____

_____

Your willingness to have God or your Higher Power take these defects is:

_____

_____

_____

_____

_____

_____

_____

_____

_____

_____

_____

Who are you without these defects? Who can you become without your defects?

_____

_____

_____

_____

_____

_____

_____

Back to trust in God or your Higher Power. What is your level of trust that they will be removed?

_____

_____

_____

_____

_____

If you do not have a lot of trust, what step can you retake to build on trust?

_____

_____

_____

_____

_____

_____

What you have been doing, in part, is grief work, and in grief work once you have said all there is to say to a person, your old addictive self, a place, a thing, or an event that is no longer in your life, the only thing left to say is "goodbye." You are now at a point in your recovery that requires you to finally let go of what is blocking you from healthy relationships. If you now have a healthy relationship with yourself and others, you will be living in new territory. It is also necessary to let go of these defects in order for you to work the remainder of the steps in an effective manner. The Seventh Step prayer also stated: "Grant me the strength as I go out from here, to do your bidding."

You know you need strength in the following areas or ways:

_____

_____

_____

_____

_____

_____

_____

_____

_____

_____

_____

_____

_____

_____

Once done you can progress to Step 8.

NOTES

NOTES

Chapter 9

Step 8

"Made a list of all persons we had harmed, and became willing to make amends to them all".

Or

"Made a list of the people, institutions, family, school personal, police that we had harmed, and became willing to let them go".

These questions may help you in making your list.

Go back to Step 4 and write down the names of all the people you hurt by what you thought or did. You discovered this information in Steps 4 and 5. When you discover the exact nature of your wrongs, and see your part in it them, you can make a realistic list of harm you have done others.

It is helpful to write out exactly want you did that was hurtful. Write down the dates, and the names of the people involved. Here you correct your wrongs by listing them and becoming willing to make amends for your past.

In Steps 1-7 you are healing your relationship with yourself and God or your Higher Power. Steps 8-9 help you heal your relationships with others. Addictive, dysfunctional, rageful, co-dependent, blaming behaviors do not make it easy to have close relationships. You are in recovery to have a better life and find some happiness in the world.

List your experiences that require making amends:

_____

_____

_____

_____

_____

_____

_____

List any amends you are not willing to make yet/ever:

_____

_____

_____

_____

_____

_____

What do you hope to gain from making amends?

_____

_____

_____

_____

_____

_____

How you believe making amends will release you from the past?

_____

_____

_____

_____

_____

_____

_____

Becoming willing is all that is asked for in this step. Willingness is a mental state of being ready, or of not holding anything back. You are also looking at giving up your attachments to blaming or believing others owe you something for what they did to you. You are not letting others off any hook if they have hurt you. But, you are simply continuing to do what you can to free *yourself* from the negative consequences for your behavior. Remember it was your inventory in Step 4, not anyone else's.

You notice you're holding back on your willingness on making amends to the following people, places, things or events:

_____

_____

_____

_____

_____

_____

_____

_____

_____

The reason you are holding back is:

_____

_____

_____

_____

_____

_____

_____

In Step 2, you became willing to believe in a power greater than yourself that would restore you to sanity. At first look, your insanity is your thinking that you can use chemicals, sex, anger, and rage with no consequences. Now you can use the step to help free you from the insane consequences of blaming others. So again, Step 8 prepares you to do more action, like make amends. I believe that this step preparing you to do the amends helps you further decide to be honest, and-, to be restored to sanity.

Here you are also considering the idea of forgiveness. This word does not always have a positive meaning. To some it has meant that the wrong done you is not significant and doesn't matter. To other it means that it is OK that wrongs were done to you. A definition of forgiveness from John James in *The Grief Recovery Handbook* states "Forgiveness is giving up the idea or the possibility of a different or better yesterday."

Since you cannot change yesterday, maybe you can give up this idea.

Which people on your list do you feel the greatest need to make amends with?

_____

_____

_____

_____

_____

_____

_____

List anyone that you want to make amends to, but you think they need to make amends to you first.

_____

_____

_____

_____

_____

_____

_____

_____

_____

_____

_____

The list you just made is important to help you notice when you are doing this work with strings attached. Remember the step is stating your amends to others, not theirs to you.

Now to go on with the work, you move to step 9.

NOTES

NOTES

Chapter 10

Step 9 –

"Made direct amends to such people wherever possible, except when to do so would injure them or others".

Or

"Went to people we had harmed whenever possible, but did not do anything to further harm ourselves of others".

Be sure you check with your sponsor, clergy person, trusted friend or counselor before doing the work. It is not about getting well at someone else's expense. With your list in hand, you may call or make appointments with the people you put on your list in Step 8. There is no need to make amends if anyone is going to get harmed. Courage is required in this step, as it takes courage to change your behavior-, and to own up to your part in the problem in the relationship. You are going against your addictive, dysfunctional tendencies, which may have been to blame or disown your responsibility.

What does making direct amends mean to you?

_____

_____

_____

_____

_____

Forgiveness has often been compared to spiritual surgery. The poison of anger, resentment, and blame is being removed with forgiveness. Distant painful memories that haunt you seem to disappear when you begin this part of your healing work. The pain of the past simply becomes the past.

How do you see forgiveness as setting you free and healing your painful memories?

_____

_____

_____

_____

_____

_____

_____

Timing and good judgment are important when taking Step 9. Once you have decided to make amends-, and are somewhat clear on your direction, it is suggested that you go over your plans with your sponsor, clergy, counselor or trusted friend prior to making your amends. This way you can be clear on exactly how you will handle it, how you will cover your part in the relationship, as well as leave what others did completely out of the communication. This process in not about getting someone to see the wrong they did to you; rather it's about becoming free from your reaction to what was done to you. Do you know for sure that you are powerless over others but that you do have power over your reaction to what they say or do to you? Do you also know that in all relationships each person plays some part in it?

What do you believe is important to understand before you make amends?

_____

_____

_____

_____

_____

_____

_____

This step requires you to make direct amends whenever possible. You must not put it off because you do not believe the time is right, or with some other excuse. Remember the purpose of the step is to clean up your side of the street, and to ensure your sobriety-, and life change. If you feel fear, go back to Step 3 and remember you have turned your will and life over to the care of the God of your understanding. If you do turn it over, then fearlessness will come about, and you will make the amends.

You are afraid of the following when you make your amends:

_____

_____

_____

_____

_____

_____

_____

_____

_____

The last part of the step cautions us with the words: "except when to do so would injury them or others."

People you might hurt include parents, girl/boy friends, teachers, police, or business owners. It is suggested you analyze the harm you did and thoroughly discuss your proposed action plan before making the amends. Sometimes simply being ready to make the amends is enough in these cases. Changing your behavior now and being consistent with the changes is how you may choose to handle some of these amends.

List the people, places, things or events that fall into the category of people you might hurt:

_____

_____

_____

_____

_____

_____

_____

Write down specifically how you think making amends will harm anyone to whom you are going to make amends:

_____

_____

_____

_____

_____

_____

_____

In some cases putting off the amends will best serve all concerned. You may not have all the information or time you need to make the amends, they may be sick, their feelings may still be raw, they may be out of town. And remember that the longer you wait to do the work the more you hurt yourself. Willingness is the key in this and in all the steps.

List the people who fall into this waiting list:

_____

_____

_____

_____

_____

_____

_____

Put down the time frame you plan to do the work in:

_____

_____

_____

_____

_____

_____

_____

Some people are good communicators and some are not. How is your communication when it comes to telling the truth about the part you played in a situation?

_____

_____

_____

_____

_____

_____

_____

_____

By simply writing down your plans you will be better able to tell your truth, and find a freedom unknown to you up to this point.

Be willing to love and forgive yourself and others.

Be clear about what you want to say and be careful not to blame others.

Take responsibility for what you are going to say.

Be willing to accept the outcome.

Don't expect any particular response.

Turn the process and the outcome over your Higher Power

Prepare your list, and if you find you are still angry or resentful, put it off and do another Step 4 on the person before you proceed with your amends to them.

Keep it simple.

This is *your* amends to them, not theirs to you.

Ask permission to make the amends.

A sample of how to state an amends is as follows:

I was (state your feelings: angry, hurt, sad, drunk, loaded, etc.) when _____ happened, and I ask your forgiveness for (name the harm done) and for anything else I may have done in the past to cause you pain. I do not intend to cause you pain again.

Or

I want you to know that I am making this amends because I understand that I hurt you. I make amends for (name the harm done) and I ask your forgiveness.

Some communication will be face to face, some on the telephone, some in e-mail or a letter. Go over with your sponsor, counselor, clergy or trusted friend how you plan to communicate the amends.

List the ways you can communicate the amends:

_____

_____

_____

_____

_____

_____

_____

When it comes time to make amends to yourself, gentleness is extremely important. Most of you have been very hard on yourself for your past behaviors. This self-judgment is counter-productive and totally unnecessary. Once again, it is important to remember that you are doing all this work to ensure your sobriety or behavioral change. Beating up on yourself is totally counterproductive.

Going back over your inventory, look for the exact nature of your wrong to yourself. When were you judgmental, harsh, blaming, living with no boundaries or taking on all aspects of a situation, and not holding others responsible for the part they played? Go over your life and get clear on these issues.

Many people have gotten a lot of benefit by looking at themselves in a mirror, making eye contact, and speaking out loud to themselves. They state the amends they owe themselves. Some have had their sponsor, clergy, counselor, or trusted friend with them during this process with wonderful results.

How do you feel now that you have completed this part of your recovery journey?

_____

_____

_____

_____

_____

_____

_____

"The Big Book of AA" and the book-, *"From Victims to Survivors"* from Alanon/ACA make promises about what the benefits are after you do Step 9. The promises include as sense of a new freedom, healthier relationships, and making better choices. Be sure to read the promises in these books.

List how your life has improved as a result of working the first 9 steps:.

_____

_____

_____

_____

_____

_____

_____

_____

_____

_____

_____

_____

_____

_____

_____

NOTES

NOTES

Chapter 11

Step 10 –

"Continued to take personal inventory and, when we were wrong, promptly admitted it".

Or

"Looked at our behavior on a regular basis, using the inventory process and, admitted our wrongs as soon as we noticed them".

Yes, this step is all about action. In fact it is action and more action. It was your actions that got you in trouble; it is your actions that keep you out of trouble as well. In Step 10 you have a tool or process where you can continue to clean up mistakes in your lives as you make them, rather than letting them stockpile or grow over time. Being free of addiction, dysfunctional behavior, rage, anger, or co-dependence does not mean you have no problems with life. It just means you are free from the effects of the dysfunctional or addictive behavior of using. Life still goes on. You are learning how to be in healthy relationships with yourself, God or your Higher Power and others. So until you master living without dysfunctional behavior, you need tools to live by and ways to clean up the harm you do to others and yourself.

Step 10 suggests you "continue to take personal inventory." So how do you do this? It really can be an easy process. Throughout the day notice your motives and behaviors towards others and yourself. If you react to someone with sideways anger (i.e., getting angry at them instead of having

your feelings, make amends to them as soon as you notice your inappropriate reaction. Then go to the person whom you have feelings about and discuss them with them. Maybe if you react with anger, you really were feeling scared or hurt. Go back to them and make amends for the anger and tell them your true feelings. The humility that you gain from this process helps you grow spiritually and personally.

What addictive, co-dependent behaviors are still active in your life?

_____

_____

_____

_____

_____

_____

_____

_____

_____

_____

How have your addictive behaviors been removed?

_____

_____

_____

_____

_____

_____

_____

_____

In Step 4 you did a complete inventory of your life prior to coming to the program. Step 10 assists you in cleaning up your problems as they come up day to day. In order for you to more easily progress, it's important to see just how far you have come.

In your progress working the first 9 steps, you are most satisfied in the following areas:

_____

_____

_____

_____

_____

You are disappointed with your progress in the following areas:

_____

_____

_____

_____

_____

_____

_____

Remember, this is a program of progress, not perfection, so by noticing where you are not progressing just gives you a benchmark on where you are, and you can then decide to take further steps to improve your life.

Meetings with people in recovery, friends, clergy, counselors, or understanding people are important to help you maintain your changes. After all, you were involved with people when you were using, and you accepted their support in keeping you in that lifestyle. Recovery relationships are the same, except in recovery there are emotional risks and vulnerabilities. Support is important to help you stay sober, clean, sane and functional.

What is going on with you to ensure you that you benefit from meetings or from talking things over with people you trust?

_____

_____

_____

_____

_____

_____

_____

_____

How have meetings with these people helped?

_____

_____

_____

_____

_____

_____

_____

_____

In Step 10 it says, "when wrong promptly admitted it." This is an extremely important concept in recovery. It means to clean up the wreckage of your present as it occurs, rather than years later. Sure, it can be seen as a leveling of your pride, but if you get a better life out of it, why not level it out? Being off of chemicals and other dysfunctional behaviors tends to clean your mind, and you grow in consciousness and understanding. By admitting your wrongs, you free yourself from guilt, shame, and remorse. These are all negative responses to life's events. You also practice Humility over and over again. Humility is not gained through repeated humiliations; rather, it is gained through your honesty. Admitting you did something wrong is different than stating "I am wrong." The statement "I am wrong" is a shame-based statement, and by working the steps, especially Steps 4 & 5, you have begun to crack the strong hold shame has had on you. So if you feel ashamed of yourself, you can work Step 10 and admit your wrong to yourself. This will release you from the pains of shame and guilt.

What is the value in promptly admitting your wrongs?

_____

_____

_____

_____

_____

_____

_____

Have you acquired the habit of daily inventory? If not, what is stopping you?

_____

_____

_____

_____

_____

_____

_____

Until now what were you doing to practice your belief in your Higher Power or God?

_____

_____

_____

_____

_____

_____

_____

How do you believe spiritual help will assist you in this ongoing inventory work?

_____

_____

_____

_____

_____

_____

What character defects still have a hold over you and how do they show up in your life?

_____

_____

_____

_____

_____

_____

_____

You resist letting these character defects go because?

_____

_____

_____

_____

_____

_____

_____

_____

_____

_____

_____

Your Higher Power's help in letting these go is beneficial in the following ways:

_____

_____

_____

_____

_____

_____

_____

The new defects of character that have shown up since you joined the program are:

_____

_____

_____

_____

_____

It's important to take an inventory of everything, good and bad. Many of you have spent a lot of time looking and living in the bad or negatives. Now is the time to explore the positives about you. If you do not see any positives, go back to Step 4 & 5 to inventory the causes and conditions that taught you to see yourself only in a negative light.

Your good qualities are:

_____

_____

_____

_____

_____

_____

_____

_____

_____

_____

_____

_____

Inventory also helps you keep in touch with reality, so that you can make better decisions. Since you are not cured of addiction, what you do have is a daily reprieve from it. This is not good news to the addict. What do you notice about the idea that you are not cured? (Cure means you can successfully put chemicals in your body with no negative consequences.)

_____

_____

_____

_____

_____

_____

_____

_____

_____

_____

_____

Growth requires constant work and awareness of your self. Inventory work can help you notice if you are returning to old behaviors or thought patterns that were a part of your old life. In what areas of life have you returned to your addictive, dysfunctional ways of doing things or living?

_____

_____

_____

_____

_____

_____

_____
_____
_____
_____
_____
_____
_____
_____

What is the importance of continuing to practice Step 3 in your life as you continue to inventory (Step 10) your life?

_____
_____
_____
_____
_____
_____
_____
_____

What is your daily ritual to help insure you will continue your new practice of daily truth-telling?

_____
_____
_____
_____
_____
_____
_____
_____

You are now ready to look at your daily communication with God, or your Higher Power of your understanding. Your daily practice is:

_____

_____

_____

_____

_____

_____

_____

_____

_____

_____

_____

_____

_____

_____

_____

_____

_____

NOTES

NOTES

Chapter 12

Step 11

"Sought through prayer and meditation to improve our conscious contact with God as we understood Him, praying only for knowledge of His will for us and the power to carry that out".

Or

"Through asking and listening to our Higher Power we improved our relationship with Him, we ask only for the knowledge of His will in our lives and that we be given the Power to carry it out.">

Let's divide the steps up and look at the many aspects of it. I really love this step as it speaks to your empowerment, and the possibilities available to you in a way the other steps do not. You will begin, "We sought through prayer and meditation to improve our conscious contact with God as we understood him." This part states that you are going to seek out something, and how you will seek it out. Seeking through prayer suggests you are going to be asking your God or your Higher Power for a way to improve your contact with him/her/it. Prayer, as explained in the earlier translations of the Bible, is an affirmation of already having the request granted. It is creating and living in the dream fulfilled. If you ask in the traditional sense you are affirming that you do not have what you are praying for, so you are coming from a position of lack.

You believe prayer is:

_____

_____

_____

_____

_____

_____

_____

Prayer has helped in your recovery in the following ways:

_____

_____

_____

_____

_____

_____

_____

Step 2 says you already have a relationship with your God or your Higher Power and you simply want to know how to improve it. So after you ask, you "meditate" or hear God's or your Higher Power's response. Meditation is not well understood in many cultures. It is simply a process of quieting yourself so you can listen to your inner wisdom, your God, or your Higher Power. Many people give up just after they start meditating because of all the loud or soft self-talk that goes on inside their heads. Some people feel very uncomfortable if they are with themselves too long. So meditation can be threatening to many people, but since Step 11 is about improving conscious contact-, with God, this step allows you to check out your willingness to stay on this path.

Meditation means this to you:

_____

_____

_____

_____

_____

_____

_____

You are aware of improving your conscious contact with God in the following ways:

_____

_____

_____

_____

_____

_____

_____

You understand your God or your Higher Power in your life today in the following ways:

_____

_____

_____

_____

Meditation is a simple process. What I present here is only a small amount of information compared to the volumes available. One way to meditate is to sit quietly with eyes opened or closed. When your eyes are closed you can tune out the surrounding distractions. Next, simply think of a problem, discomfort or question you have, get clear about what it is, and then let it go.

Begin to focus on your breathing, and just breathe in and out. If you notice you are thinking of something other than your breathing, just go back to focusing on your breathing. Do this for about 3-5 minutes to start. Shorten your time if it is too long.

Another good way to start is to sit quietly and place your focus on a candle about 45 degrees above you on a shelf. This eye position automatically produces the trance state of Alpha consciousness.

If it is very difficult for you to sit quietly, then the following will be beneficial. Find an open room or yard space. With your eyes open decide on a circle distance you can walk in. Keeping your eyes just barely open, slowly begin to walk in the circle, focusing on taking one step at a time. Giving your problem, issue, question up to your God or your Higher Power and wait to hear what shows up for you. Quiet music is also helpful to some. You can do spot-check meditation during a busy day as well. Go to a bathroom for 3-5 minutes when you feel tense or hurried. Focus on your breathing when you are in a tight/tense situation, and take in 4-8 deep breaths[,] doing anything to help you defocus from your anxieties or problems.

The best meditation practice for you is:

_____

_____

_____

_____

_____

_____

_____

_____

_____

When you think of meditating you feel/think:

_____

_____

_____

_____

_____

_____

_____

Another way of meditating is to find a broken tree, plant, or some living or dead thing and focus on the most broken place on it. Then ask why this thing is beautiful even though it is broken. Then see how you can apply this answer to your problem or concern.

_____

_____

_____

_____

_____

How does your sense of "self" or pride get in the way of your relationship with your God or Higher Power.

_____

_____

_____

_____

_____

_____

_____

The next part of Step 11 is "Praying only for knowledge of his will for us." Now you are going to address your trust in your God or your Higher Power. The step is asking you to have total reliance on this power source to guide you to a higher will than yours. When you were using, rageful, blaming, or acting out, this made no sense. But now you are in a different place. You are operating from a higher consciousness. You are becoming more God-conscious.

From your past experiences, how have you learned to trust your God or Higher Power?

_____

_____

_____

_____

_____

_____

Your relationship with you God or Higher Power has improved in the following ways:

_____

_____

_____

_____

_____

_____

So far you have seen that God or your Higher Power is a good, kind, living entity. It is awesome and exciting to realize that you can have an abundant, wonderful life. Bill W. and Dr. Bob, the co-founders of AA, seemed to believe that an abundant life could be obtained for the asking when they wrote, "We found that God does not make too hard terms with those who seek him. To us, the Realm of Spirit is broad, roomy, all-inclusive; never exclusive or forbidding to those who earnestly seek Him. It is open, we believe, to all men/women."

What are your feelings about what is written above?

_____

_____

_____

_____

_____

_____

_____

_____

_____

_____

_____

_____

Your understanding of your God's or Higher Power's will is now:

_____

_____

_____

_____

_____

_____

When you are given new information, or want to make any changes, you need energy to carry out these new changes-, "and for the power to carry that out."

This step states that you will be given what is necessary to transform your God's or Higher Power's will into your lives. This type of guarantee is powerful. So again you are being asked to trust that power. How willing are you to allow change into your life now compared to your willingness prior to working this step?

_____

_____

_____

_____

_____

_____

_____

_____

Your current level of faith in your God or Higher Power is:

_____

_____

_____

_____

_____

_____

_____

If you seek through prayer and meditation to improve your conscious contact with God as you understand Him/Her, and pray only for knowledge of His/Her will for you and for the power to carry this out, you will be sure to find happiness. It will also lead to closure and fulfillment in all areas of your life.

This moves you to Step 12, where you will acknowledge your changes and share them with others and live a new life.

NOTES

NOTES

Chapter 13

Step 12

"Having had a spiritual awakening as the result of these steps, we tried to carry this message to others and to practice these principals in all our affairs".

Or

"We had a spiritual awakening because we worked the steps, we carried our massage learned by doing the work to others and we then practiced these new behaviors in all our activities".

You are not at the end of your journey; you are simply on a higher plane. You are not cured, but you do have significantly more life skills available to you, and you can feel honest joy. Again, cure would mean you have altered your physical condition.

Remember that your body and your mind are wired differently than others', so you have the propensity to become addicted again if you do not practice a new way of living and thinking. You have not altered your physical condition. Rather, you have altered your mental and spiritual self, and your sanity has been restored as it related to your drinking, drugging, acting-out, or co-dependent behavior. The Big Book of AA states that a spiritual awakening or experience is a personality change sufficient to help you recover from your addiction.

You have transformed or changed yourself in the following ways:

_____

_____

_____

_____
_____
_____
_____

In Step 1, you changed in the following ways:

_____
_____
_____
_____
_____
_____
_____
_____
_____
_____

In Step 2, you changed in the following ways:

_____
_____
_____
_____
_____
_____

In Step 3, you changed in the following ways:

_____

_____

_____

_____

_____

_____

_____

In Step 4, you changed in the following ways:

_____

_____

_____

_____

_____

_____

_____

In Step 5, you changed in the following ways:

_____

_____

_____

_____

_____

In Step 6, you changed in the following ways:

_____

_____

_____

_____

_____

_____

_____

In Step 7, you changed in the following ways:

_____

_____

_____

_____

_____

_____

In Step 8, you changed in the following ways:

_____

_____

_____

_____

_____

_____

_____

In Step 9, you changed in the following ways:

_____

_____

_____

_____

_____

_____

_____

In Step 10, you changed in the following ways:

_____

_____

_____

_____

_____

_____

_____

In Step 11, you changed in the following ways:

_____

_____

_____

_____

_____

_____

_____

If you changed yourself as a result of taking these steps, it is seems only natural that you would be interested in progressing further. You have experienced something and you now have a different life experience. Your experiences have given you something to share. It is your message of change that you can carry to others. It's not a theory; it's a report of action taken.

Working the steps is like the story of the transformation of a caterpillar to a butterfly. The caterpillar does not know that it is going to be a butterfly. Every part of its death and rebirth must be experienced. It only recognizes its transformation after it has emerged as changed and is free to fly. A girl once noticed a cocoon on a bush in her yard. As she started to pull it from the bush and throw it away, she noticed the end was opening and a butterfly was struggling to escape. In an effort to help the emerging butterfly, she took it inside and very carefully cut the cocoon away. The butterfly feebly crawled from the open cocoon but within a few hours died. It needed the strength it would have gained from the struggle to free itself in order to survive in the outside world. Just like the butterfly, you need to gain strength through hard work. Your working the steps is helping you develop your strength to live a strong, healthy life.

You are strong in these areas of your life now as a result of working the steps:

_____

_____

_____

_____

_____

_____

The recovery message you have to offer other is:

_____

_____

_____

_____

_____

_____

Your current relationships to family and friends have improved in the following ways:

_____

_____

_____

_____

_____

_____

As a result of working your program you feel better about yourself in the following ways:

_____

_____

_____

_____

_____

_____

_____

Because of working Steps 4 and 5 you got free from your attachments to your negative self-judgment. You are now free from:

_____

_____

_____

_____

_____

_____

_____

In what ways will you carry your message of hope and recovery?

_____

_____

_____

_____

_____

_____

Therapy: After Care Group, Group Therapy, Counseling, Hypnosis, Solution Focused Therapy, Emotional Freedom Techniques, Thought Field Therapy etc.

_____

_____

_____

_____

_____

_____

Peer Support; The appropriate 12 Step group Palmer Drug Abuse Program, AA, NA, CA, SLAA, SA, GA, DA, EA, ACA, CODA, Alanon, Ala-teen, Gam-Anon, (SMART Recovery) = Self Management And Recovery Training(compatible with 12 step programs but not spiritual in nature), Rational Recovery (opposed to 12 step groups and not spiritual in nature), Women/Men for Sobriety etc.

_____

_____

_____

_____

_____

_____

Church Group

_____

_____

_____

_____

_____

NOTES

NOTES

Chapter 14

Challenging and Changing Negative Self-defeating Beliefs

The next step for ongoing, life-long recovery is in challenging and changing negative, self-defeating core beliefs. Looking back at the cycle of addiction you noticed that the cycle begins with your beliefs. What you believe defines you because you give beliefs power over you. But in reality beliefs are not real; they are only thoughts. Beliefs are thoughts about self or others. Beliefs guide you in a particular direction, or define how you react, respond, act, talk or behave. Challenging long-held beliefs is as difficult as step work. It's helpful to do this with a counselor, trusted friend, clergy, or sponsor. What this work will help you do is to take a jack hammer to the foundation of beliefs you have been standing on, and then enable you to create a new foundation of belief to base your new life on.

So let's get started. I'll lay it out, and then proceed to the forms that follow.

(A) The first step in this process is to define one event in your early life history or in the present day. We will use events and beliefs around using drugs, alcohol or acting out.

(B) Then you will identify the beliefs that come up, or the self-talk that accompanies the beliefs about yourself.

(C) Next you will define the feelings that go with the belief. This A + B + C process happens many times throughout the day. But now you are going to do something most people don't know they can do or just don't do.

(D) You are now going to challenge or dispute your belief. In order for this dispute to work it must be strong or convincing enough that you can believe it and it must be strong enough to shatter the old belief. Remember, you are going against authority and, in this case, it is your belief about you that is the authority. You are challenging yourself. It takes work and may seem odd to do. Many people get tired, or uncomfortable, and want to go to sleep. They say that it just won't work. Some even get angry at the thought of challenging an existing belief. If you are willing to stick with it you can rid yourself of any limiting belief about yourself you want.

(E) Once the belief has been successfully disputed, create a new belief in place of the old one.

(F) Then notice how you feel about yourself with the new belief in place.

(G) Next tell the truth about the event that you started this process with. The truth is that it occurred, nothing more. All of the self-talk is your created reaction to the event. Just because something happens does not make anything about you. It is always about itself, not you. However, your reaction to any event is always about you, not it. These ideas are not only true, they also are empowering. Just think, if you created your problems, then you can fix or resolve them as well. This is true power, or the right use of power.

A. The Event – Briefly describe what happened and what was said that you have feelings about now.

_____

_____

_____

_____

_____

_____

_____

_____

_____

_____

B. Describe your negative self-talk. Questions, etc. (like, why did they do that or say that, what did I do to cause them to do or say that, etc.)

_____

_____

_____

_____

_____

Now describe or name the negative statements you use about you. Look for "I'm" statements like "I'm bad," "I'm stupid," etc., that relate to the event.

_____

_____

_____

_____

_____

_____

Now look for your personal life mandate, like "I will always be bad," "I will never get any better," "I should have done," "I ought to have/should have said/done and because I did not I'm _____."

_____

_____

_____

_____

_____

_____

_____

C. Now how do you feel as a result of the beliefs? (Happy, sad, confused, upset, angry, resentful, etc.)

Now you have your A+B+C's written down. This is what goes on in most people's minds every day, and they never question it. You have been trained to not question your negative self-talk, and you assume that it is true. You are domesticated to believe that just because someone says or does something to you, you deserve it. So in these columns go back through the negative self-talk and begin to challenge it. Remember, you agreed to the talk when you stated it, even though you were probably not aware of the fact that you were agreeing to it when it occurred. No one was there to help you confront it or challenge it when it happened, but now you are here to challenge it and get a new perspective on it.

Examples of disputes are the following:

(1) Just because my father hit me does not make me a bad person

(2) Just because my mother said I was stupid for doing something does not make me stupid;

(3) Even if others don't like this or that about me, I am not unlikable, etc.

D. Dispute the negative self-talk.

_____

_____

_____

_____

_____

_____

Now create a new belief for each statement you disputed. You can use the following examples or something better:

(1)I'm intelligent-,

(2) I'm good, even if my behavior is not so good-,

(3) I'm smart-,

(4) I can amount to anything I choose to be as long as I work toward it, etc.

E. Now notice your new feelings about you as a result of changing your belief:

_____

_____

_____

_____

_____

_____

_____

_____

_____

_____

F. Now tell the truth about the event. The only truth is that the event happened.

_____

_____

_____

_____

_____

_____

_____

_____

_____

_____

_____

_____

_____

After you do this exercise go back to the original event and notice the new way you have of looking on it. If it still feels uncomfortable you can redo the exercise. Keep disputing the negative self-talk until it's gone or does not generate uncomfortable feelings.

Notice your investment in the discomfort associated with the negative self-talk. Sometimes people get what are called "secondary gains" or they get to play the victim longer by holding onto the old way of viewing a situation. How about you? This process works 100% of the time for those who work it. It is not theory; it is practical reality. Do this exercise every time you tell yourself some limiting thing about yourself. When you do your 4th, 5th, 8th or even in the 10th step, it will work to give you a new perspective.

This process, like the 12 steps, can become a part of how you handle life now. I maintain that as long as people have effective tools to deal with life, they choose life over some addictive, dysfunctional, life-harming behavior.

Your final task is to say goodbye to your grief and pain or any dysfunctional behavior in your life. This process works very effectively for all loss issues, whether it is a death or non-death-related loss.

NOTES

NOTES

Chapter 15

Grief/Loss and Life Transition Process

This work is also meant to become a part of your life-long living skills. One thing everyone is going to experience in life is loss. You are generally never taught how to experience it in a productive way. Many people never had any specific positive lessons on how to say goodbye to any relationship that is no longer in their life. In addiction recovery, most people are glad to get clean, sober, stop acting out, to release and let go of their anger or rageful behaviors, and their depression. Leaving the addiction behind is a loss, and if you learn how to manage losses, any uncomfortable feelings pass through you in a most natural way.

As you experience loss, if there is an adaptive way to have the feelings and then release them, the pain does not have to become overwhelming or last a lifetime.

First let's look at the messages given to many people early in life that teach how to grieve or how to repress the feelings associated with experiencing loss. These are generalizations; while they apply to many, they may not apply to you. When I'm talking about lessons, I'm talking about what was said and done when a loss occurred. Most of you were not given any specific talk about how to grieve or express these feelings. Many times you were taught to repress the feelings with messages like:

"Go to your room and cry, but not out here. You will upset _____," or "Keep a stiff upper lip." When you had something that was lost or stolen, the messages were often "You can just get another one" or "It can be replaced." In death there were messages like, "They are at home with God, so why are you so sad?" or "They are better off." If the death was suicide, many times the rule was silence, and the 'Just don't talk about it" rule was in place. Maybe you believed you had a part to play in the loss so you got caught up in your own questions, like "What could I have done differently, better?" which helps you avoid your feelings.

List what you were taught directly or indirectly about death or loss:

_____

_____

_____

_____

_____

_____

_____

_____

_____

_____

_____

_____

_____

_____

_____

When you are making your timeline loss graph, be sure to assign a message given for each loss you identify. These messages mold you in how to experience these events. These early messages set you up for your adolescent and adult ways of experiencing your feelings associated with loss. These patterns are what you bring into all areas of your lives.

_____

_____

_____

_____

_____

_____

_____

_____

_____

_____

_____

_____

As a result of these messages you learn how to repress your feelings. As feelings will always show up, directly or indirectly, you learn to develop behaviors that may help you medicate the feelings but do not resolve them. Some people medicate by doing better in school, doing poorly in school, acting out with anger, rage, addictive behaviors, depression, suicide attempts, cutting on one's self, eating disorders or excelling in an activity or school. What did you do?

_____

_____

_____

_____

_____

_____

_____

_____

_____

_____

How have you learned to repress your feelings and then repress expressing them?

_____

_____

_____

_____

_____

_____

_____

The next things to identify are any accidents or illnesses that occurred 3 to 6 months after each loss. Some people have many, but some have only a few or none. Like the work you have been doing, it's important to see how you have avoided your feelings by creating these things in your life. If you have throat, neck, or head accidents or illnesses, you could be avoiding speaking up about something, or being inflexible, or not being willing to acknowledge your intuition or your spiritual connection. If the problems show up in the heart or stomach, genital area or legs, you could be repressing feelings of love or dislike, or have low self-esteem. You may have your feelings of worth threatened, or be unable to fully express your creative nature, or feel blocked in your creativity or unable to move forward in one area of your life.

Identify your accidents or illness and how they affected your body:

_____

_____

_____

_____

_____

_____

_____

_____

_____

_____

_____

The next step in this awakening process is to identify types of losses in your life, and what the losses meant to you. Most of us are only aware of the loss, not what it means to us. The meaning of the loss is what you are working with here. So I'll list some events that involve loss, and you add your own: Death, divorce, graduation, getting a job, losing a job, getting a boyfriend/girlfriend, losing a boyfriend/girlfriend, separation, losing a best friend to a move or fight, loss of control over a behavior (anger/rage/acting out), doing something you regretful or feeling bad because of a drunk or a high, loss due to theft, loss due to (incest, sexual abuse, rape), loss of innocence, loss due to (physical, verbal, spiritual, emotional, financial) abuse.

Add/identify your own specific losses now:

_____

_____

_____

_____

_____

With each loss event there is an emotional loss as well. For example, if your father hits you and tells you that you will not amount to anything, the loss may include loss of safety, security, love, personal boundaries, self-worth (depending of how you internalized what he did and said). Identifying these meanings is new behavior to most people. Many say it's tough to do this, and I say, do you want to recover? If you do want to recover do the work anyway, even if it's tough. It's your life at stake. If you find it hard to care for your life, then define the loss there. Is it loss of self-esteem, self-worth, caring, self-love, self-respect? If this is the case, you may want to refer back to Chapter 13 and do that exercise again.

Another example of the emotions attached to loss could be loss of innocence, choices, ability to speak for one's self, loss of control, loss due to terror, fear or abandonment. It is important to identify these emotional losses as they may appear as a pattern in your life. Like Fritz Pearl said, "You will repeat what you do not complete."

Now you will move on to the next part of this powerful process.

(1) Make a time line showing every loss in your life

(2) Attach the messages taught with each loss

(3) Attach the behaviors you developed to repress the feelings

(4) Identify the accidents and illness used to further repress your feelings-.

This time line is for your entire life. So start at birth and end the graph with today.

Birth   Today

Draw a vertical line down off of the horizontal line to indicate the severity of the loss. Then on the horizontal line put the loss event, and then put a word or two on the vertical line to define what the loss meant to you. The length of the vertical line states the severity of the loss for you. You are the only one who really knows the severity of any loss. Well meaning peoples statements like "I know how you feel" are really just attempts to be kind but they really do not know how you feel. Its OK, you never really know how anyone feels. We can only guess or know how we feel when the event/loss happens to us. When you complete the above, put the following misinformation down that you were taught (not in a obvious lesson but rather in terms of a behavioral lesson like what people around you expected of you) in order to suppress the feelings, like: grieve alone, don't talk, don't trust, don't feel, replace the loss, keep your feelings to yourself, etc.

The message you were taught in order to repress you feelings were:

_____

_____

_____

_____

_____

_____

_____

_____

_____

The behaviors you did to help you repress the feelings: i.e. act out, drink, drug, get angry, isolate, become rageful, oppositional defiant, become better in school, did poorly in class, become super involved in school or private activities etc.

_____

_____

_____

_____

_____

_____

The accidents that occurred 3-6 months after each loss: some people have them some don't just look and identify.

_____

_____

_____

_____

_____

_____

The illnesses that occurred 3-6 months after the loss: Some people develop illness some don't, just identify.

_____

_____

_____

_____

Once all this work is done, share it with a sponsor, counselor, friend, therapist, sponsor, or teacher who you can trust to let you have your truth. It may be emotionally painful to go through the process and seem useless, but remember, this process like all others in the book are reports of actions taken to produce specific results, in this case to become free of the pain of the past.

You and your sharing partner (therapist, minister, trusted friend, sponsor) will begin to notice patterns of behavior, losses, messages, and coping skills. This is a blueprint of your life today. It will show you how you have been trained to experience life. It is valuable information you're discovering now.

Once the information on the graph has been read, you will notice which losses have an emotion attached to them and which ones have no emotional charges on them. Pick the losses which still have emotional charges associated with them to work on. It may help to prioritize them or rate them from 1 on down to the last one. Once they have been prioritized, pick one to work on first. The following process will be repeated for each loss you want to complete.

Draw another horizontal line across the page. Identify the person, place, thing or event that this work is about. Then draw vertical lines above the horizontal line to indicate the positives about this relationship and vertical lines below the horizontal line to indicate the negative associated with this relationship. Go through the relationship from its beginning to today. If the person or event is no longer in your life, indicate the positives and negatives with this absence.

Now we will address some potentially sensitive areas for people. In looking at the following 2 categories of undelivered communications look at your willingness to be free from the pain of the past. Amends are what you owe someone or something for anything negative or hurtful you did, thought or said. If someone tried to make up for a wrong they did and you discounted them or did not accept it, this would be something on the amends list. An example of an amends statement might be, "I held this _____ against you and am now ready to let it go." "I am sorry for holding on to it for so long and I am changing my behaviors now."

As far as forgiveness goes I will begin with a definition I heard: "Forgiveness is releasing the possibility of a different or better outcome as it relates to the past or present." You can look at whatever was done to you by the person, place, thing or event you identified to work on and put everything they did on the list and become ready to let them off the hook for it. Resentment or re-feeling old hurts keeps you attached to the event. Grief is letting go vs. holding on to something. An example would be "I forgive you for abandoning me. I know you did your best."

Amends: You owe them for what you did to them that is negative or un-accepting.

Examples: Not accepting who you are/were, refusing to let go and move on, blamed them for your problems, made them responsible for your happiness, pain, etc.

Forgiveness: Remember that grief is a reaction to what is no longer in your life. If you do not or will not let it go, you cannot grieve. If you're willing to forgive but find it hard then do these exercises first.

(1) Write done all the benefits or what you get to avoid doing or being if you do not forgive. Examples would be you get to avoid closeness, responsibility, relationship, etc.

(2) Write down what it costs you to withhold forgiveness. Examples would be peace of mind, taking your power back or boundary development. Finally, if the cost outweighs the benefit, it will usually be easy to let it go, but if the benefit outweighs' the cost, then stop the grief work, and move into to anger/pain resolution work, and then come back to the grief work.

Once this is done then you are ready for the final step. This final process is where you get to finally say everything you ever wanted to say to the person, place, thing or event that is no longer in your life. It is important to remember to connect with the feelings vs. just the information. If all these categories do not apply just write down what does apply. If there are additional categories, then put them down as well.

I'd suggest you begin with a positive intent statement where you take responsibility for your part in this process.

"I am writing this letter to express my feelings in an honest manner with the desire to let them go, and to let you go as well."

Anger

_____

_____

_____

_____

_____

_____

Hurt

_____

_____

_____

_____

_____

_____

Pain

_____

_____

_____

Amends

_____

_____

_____

_____

_____

_____

_____

Forgiveness

_____

_____

_____

_____

_____

_____

This is want you want to keep

_____

_____

_____

_____

_____

_____

_____

Thank you, love you for

_____

_____

_____

_____

_____

_____

Anything else you want to say

_____

_____

_____

_____

_____

_____

Goodbye

_____

_____

_____

_____

_____

Repeat these things until you feel complete, or all the emotion is expressed. If something comes up later, just say what needs to be said, then say goodbye again. Every type of loss can be completed. There is nothing that has to keep you in pain for the rest of your life.

Once this is done, read the next instruction and do the exercise.

Sit quietly where you will not be disturbed. Close your eyes and imagine you are in a very safe place. In this safe place tell yourself that you are feeling relaxed and going to a deep part of your mind where you feel very, very safe and secure. Now count down from 10 to 1 very slowly. Once you get to 1, visualize yourself in a place that supports you in its color, sounds and surroundings. Now image that person, place, thing or event you have just worked on is approaching you out of a fog. As they get closer, you notice you are at eye level or on equal terms. Notice that it or they are holding a gift for you. The gift represents a better life because the situation happened exactly the way it happened. As they get closer you notice that you are also walking toward them as well. When you are very close to each other, you stop. See them giving the gift to you and you taking it from them. Now take them to a very special healing place in your heart that you have prepared for them. This is not about forgetting; it's about being able to remember. Once they are in the place you have prepared for them, leave them there, knowing you may return to visit whenever you want. Now take the gift they gave you and go to a very special, safe place in you heart you have prepared for you. Once in this environment, open the gift. Stay here until you are absolutely clear about why your life is better because the event happened exactly the way it happened. Did you get strength, completeness, tenacity, or did you develop some skill or knowledge? Whatever it is when you get it, claim it and then open you eyes and you are finished.

Breathe in the new reality, knowing that you are now free to remember the event with sadness or joy. You choose. Like I said, this work is not about forgetting; it's about how you will remember or live with the events in your life.

If some other thing comes up later that you wish to say or share with them, say it and then say goodbye again. Do this as many times as you wish. After all, it's your life and your experience. Now you can manage it more effectively.

This or other programs of recovery do not really promise a better life. Rather they promise that you have effective tools for living regardless of what happens to you in life.

~ The Beginning ~

NOTES

NOTES

Young, Sober & Free by Shelly Marshall

Women for Sobriety by Jean Kirkpatrick

If you are a survivor of sexual abuse, incest, physical abuse, rape or other trauma and you are working with a competent therapist, coach, trained minister etc. look into working with a skilled therapeutic massage therapist for non-sexual, non-violent touch to release the body memories. (Remember not all mental health professionals, MD's, PhD's, Ministers, Counselors know that the mind has a body and not all Massage Therapist or Body Workers know that the body has a mind).

Body, Mind and Soul are connected.

Have a good life: i.e. use the tools here in this and other self help books to

gain the skills for living a clean, sober and addiction free life

regardless of what happen to you in your life.

66835966R00098

Made in the USA
San Bernardino, CA
16 January 2018